WED CEREMONIES

Planning
Your
Special
Day

JO PACKHAM

A Sterling\Chapelle Book
Sterling Publishing Co., Inc. New York

Jo Packham, author

Trice Boerens, illustrator

Tina Annette Brady, designer

Sandra Durbin Chapman, editor

Margaret Shields Marti, editor

The author would like to thank the following for permission to
reprint: "Rite for Celebrating Marriage During Mass (Marriage
between two Catholics)" from *Celebrating Marriage: Preparing the
Wedding Liturgy* by Paul Covino. Reprinted by permission of
Pastoral Press.

Library of Congress Cataloging–in–Publication Data

Packham, Jo.
    Wedding ceremonies : planning your special day / Jo Packham
      p. cm.
    "A Sterling/Chapelle book"
    Includes index
    ISBN 0-8069-8834-7
    1. Weddings—Planning I. Title.
HQ745.P35 1993   92–44207
395V.22—dc20   CIP

10 9 8 7 6 5 4 3 2

Published by Sterling Publishing Company, Inc.

387 Park Avenue South, New York, N.Y. 10016

© 1993 by Chapelle Ltd.

Distributed in Canada by Sterling Publishing

C/o Canadian Manda Group, P.O. Box 920, Station U

Toronto, Ontario, Canada M8Z 5P9

Distributed in Great Britain and Europe by Cassell PLC

Villiers House, 41/47 Strand, London WC2N 5JE, England

Distributed in Australia by Capricorn Link Ltd.

P.O.Box 665, Lane Cove, NSW 2066

Manufactured in the United States of America

Sterling ISBN 0-8069-8834-7

To Judy and Michael:

Here is to the two of you
and to beginnings that know no end.

Contents

Introduction   7

Ceremony Planning   8

Types of Ceremonies   9

Choosing the Church Officiant   27

Ceremony Styles   30

Symbolic Ceremonies   47

Special Circumstances
Related to the Ceremony   50

Ceremony Vows   53

Ceremony Music   57

Ceremony Sites   66

Ceremony Seating   75

Ceremony Programs   79

Marriage License   81

The Ceremony Rehearsal   83

The Rehearsal Dinner   90

The Ceremony Timetable   92

Receiving Line for all Ceremonies 103

Ceremony Transportation   104

Ceremony Parking   108

Index   110

*Marriage is the golden ring in a chain
whose beginning is a glance and whose
ending is eternity.*

Kahlil Gibran

Introduction

"Somewhere in the chain, sometimes
placed early in the succession of links,
sometimes later, is the wedding ceremony.
A ceremony is one whose ritual, whose
symbolism, and whose tradition create a
connection that has lasted for centuries
among all of those who have married and
who will marry in the future. It not only
touches you, the bride and the groom, but
has a quiet and lasting impact on all of
those who share the moment with you."

This impact is why it is so important
to make your ceremony as perfect for
the two of you and for those you love as
it can possibly be. With careful planning,
you will create a memory and build a
love that extends beyond the span of
days and years and continues forever.

Ceremony Planning

Your wedding day is probably one of the most important days of your life, one of the richest experiences you and your beloved will ever share. Like many couples today, you will want your ceremony to be laced with tradition, to convey the importance of the commitment you have made to one another, and to be filled with the personal touches that show the qualities and individualities of the two of you.

To ensure that you will have the ceremony that you have always dreamed of, you will want to plan carefully. You will want to decide between the two of you exactly what type of ceremony you want and then make an appointment to speak to your minister, priest, rabbi, or judge as soon as possible. Discuss the significance of the vows you will recite; what, if any, individual changes or additions you would like; and what each of you feels is important for the ceremony to express about yourselves, your families, your beliefs, and the marriage you have planned.

# Types of Ceremonies

ROMAN CATHOLIC

Marriage is considered a lifelong commitment in the Catholic Church and is one of their seven sacraments. Because of the importance placed on marriage, almost every parish requires the couple to participate in pre-marital counseling in order to prepare for their new roles and responsibilities. It is advised that you contact the parish priest at least six months before the wedding date. Prenuptial counseling will generally begin two months later. Your wedding preparation programs consist of: (1) Evenings for the Engaged, (2) personality testing and evaluation sessions, and (3) instructions in the faith. If the two of you are not well-known to the priest, both will be required to submit two affidavits–obtained from either the parents, close relatives, or friends–attesting to your freedom to enter into marriage. You will also need a recent issue of your baptismal certificate, one that has been reissued not later than six months prior to the wedding day. Copies of the first Holy Communion and confirmation certificates will also be required.

The Banns, a public proclamation of an approaching marriage, are published in the church bulletin or read aloud three Sundays prior to the day of the ceremony. The Banns are announced only when both parties are Catholic and are done so in order that anyone who knows of a reason why the marriage should not take place can declare it to the priest.

Traditionally, Catholic couples wed in the bride's church, but this is not a requirement. The church prefers that all Catholic couples marry in a Nuptial Mass because of the importance this celebration brings to the occasion. Ceremonies are usually scheduled on Saturday; are held during the day before six o'clock; and are not permitted on Holy Thursday, Good Friday, Holy Saturday, or during Mass. Any exceptions must receive special dispensation.

If either party has been married before, a second marriage is permitted in the Catholic Church, as long as the party involved goes through the annulment process. Each diocese has different procedures; one needs to allow approximately one year to complete the process. The Catholic annulment is not a legal divorce.

The Catholic Church has three traditional marriage rites. The Rite of Marriage during Mass is generally used when both participants are Catholic. The Rite of Marriage outside Mass is appropriate for a Catholic marrying a person who is a member of another Christian faith and the Rite of Marriage used when a Catholic marries a person who is not a Christian vary slightly from the Rite of Marriage below. The differences can be noted and explained during your premarriage consultation.

Rite for celebrating marriage during Mass

1. *Gathering and entrance rites*
- a. Gathering of the assembly
- b. Procession
- c. Greeting
- d. Penitential rite
- e. Gloria
- f. Opening prayer

2. *Liturgy of the word*
- a. Old Testament reading
- b. Responsorial Psalm
- c. New Testament reading
- d. Gospel acclamation
- e. Gospel
- f. Homily

3. *Marriage rite*
- a. Address and statement of intentions
- b. Consent and exchange of vows
- c. Blessing and exchange of rings
- d. General intercession
- e. Preparation of the gifts
- f. Eucharistic prayer
- g. Lord's Prayer
- h. Nuptial blessing
- i. Sign of peace
- j. Breaking of the bread
- k. Communion
- l. Prayer after communion

4. *Concluding rite*
   a. Blessing
   b. Dismissal
   c. Recessional.

A voluntary offering given to the church should conform to the amount spent on the overall celebration.

PROTESTANT

With so many different denominations, each having its own practices and traditions, it is impossible to discuss all of the available options. You, the bride and groom, will need to discuss church regulations, practices, and personal wants with the clergy member of the house of worship you select.

Most Protestant ceremonies are based on the *Book Of Common Prayer* and the following list will give you an idea of the basic ceremony:

1. Music/processional
2. Welcome
3. Prayer of blessing
4. Readings (sometimes from the Scriptures or may be ones you have selected)
5. Giving in marriage (affirmation by parents)
6. Congregational responses
7. Exchange of vows
8. Exchange of rings
9. Celebration of the Lord's Supper

10. Lighting of the unity candle
11. Benediction
12. Recessional.

EASTERN ORTHODOX

The Eastern Orthodox Church is similar to the Roman Catholic Church. The leadership of the Eastern Orthodox Church is the patriarch instead of the pope. The wedding ceremony is very similar to the Roman Catholic ceremony with the differences discussed below:

1. The priest places crowns on the heads of the bride and groom which are exchanged three times. The repetition of three, represents the Holy Trinity, which has great significance in the Eastern Orthodox Church.

2. Wedding rings are blessed and then exchanged by the bride and groom three times again to honor the Holy Trinity. The rings are then placed on the right hands.

3. Lit candles are held during the ceremony symbolizing the light of the Lord.

After a Gospel reading, the two of you share a cup of wine, each drinking three times. The congregation sings "God Grant Them Many Years," and you walk hand in hand around the ceremonial table three times.

You are both required to fast, make confession, and receive Holy Communion on the Sunday before your wedding date. For interfaith marriages, only the Orthodox member receives Holy Communion. One of your witnesses must be Eastern Orthodox.

The wedding ceremony is held in a church during daylight hours and Mass is not celebrated. The vows are said in front of a sanctuary with a nearby table which holds a Bible, cross, chalice of wine, candles, and flowers.

Interfaith marriages are permitted as long as either the bride or groom is Eastern Orthodox or both are baptized Christians.

Second marriages are permitted but the couple must satisfy the individual requirements of the church.

JEWISH

According to Jewish tradition, marriage is a sanctification of life, a consecration of self toward noble ends. It is a spiritual relationship sanctioned by society and sanctified by religion.

The Jewish faith has three denominations. The Orthodox is traditional and very strict, the Conservative is less strict, and the Reformed is lenient.

Variations occur among the three Jewish denominations but the wedding ceremony follows some basic guidelines. There are three main components: (1) the ketubbah or wedding contract, (2) the ring, and (3) the huppah, a canopy which symbolizes the bridal chamber and denotes the unity of the bridal couple.

Prior to the ceremony
1. *Oyfrufn:*
    a. The groom is honored by being called up to the reading of the Torah in the synagogue. This takes place at services in the synagogue on the Sabbath preceding the marriage. The synagogue officials should be notified and the groom, his family, the bride and her family should all be present. Following the service, it is the custom for the parents of the groom to provide kiddush for members of the congregation and their guests.
    b. After the groom recites the final blessings, sweets (candy and raisins) are thrown at him to symbolize a sweet life.

2. *Fasting:* It is traditional to fast during the entire day of the wedding until the reception.

3. *Tenaim:* This is a legal document signed by the bride and groom before the ceremony.

4. *Kinyan:* This is the process whereby the groom agrees to fulfill his obligations as stated in the ketubbah. He takes a handkerchief or something offered by the rabbi as a symbol of acceptance in front of the witnesses who sign the ketubbah.

5. *Bedeken:* The ushers dance around the groom as he approaches the bride. The groom lifts the bride's veil while the rabbi recites a phrase.

The ceremony
1. *Processional:* No order is fixed by Jewish law but the traditional sequence can be seen in the diagram on page 100.

2. *Circling the groom:* The bride circles the groom two to thirteen times. Often both mothers will join you.

3. *Procedure:*
    a. Recite Psalms 118: 26-29
    b. Sing medieval hymn
    c. Blessing over wine
    d. You both drink from the goblet
    e. Groom puts ring on your right index finger.

4. *Digression:*
    a. This statement legalizes the marriage.
    b. After the marriage contract is read, it is presented to you and you are responsible for it.
    c. The Seven Blessings are recited by honored guests.

5. *Breaking the glass:* The groom stamps on a glass at the conclusion of the ceremony.

6. The bride and groom are greeted with cries of "Mazel tov!" (Good luck!)

7. *Recessional:* The order of the recession may vary, but, traditionally, it is led by the bride and groom. The traditional sequence can be seen in the diagram on page 102.

8. *Yihud:* It is customary for you both to retreat to a private room for solitude and break your fast together. Traditionally, the marriage is consummated at this time.

Rabbis from most denominations will not perform an interfaith ceremony. The non-Jewish person is required to be converted.

The wedding ceremony cannot take place on the Sabbath, during Passover, or on other holy days and most ceremonies are held in synagogues but this is not a strict requirement. Both Orthodox and Conservative ceremonies are performed in Hebrew or Aramaic only.

The ceremony is held under a marriage canopy, the huppah. It is usually made of silk or velvet and is sometimes covered with flowers. The bride, the groom, and the rabbi are always under the huppah during the ceremony. The bride stands on the groom's right and the rabbi faces them. If it is large enough to accommodate them, the parents of both you and the groom should also stand under the huppah. The maid-of-honor should be on your right and the groom's best man on his left. The attendants do not join you but line up in single file on either side of the canopy; see page 101.

During the ceremony, the rabbi stands next to a small table covered in white and set with cups of ritual wine and a glass, frequently wrapped in white silk or a napkin.

The Orthodox and Conservative Jews require the ring to be a plain gold band without gems. During the ceremony, it is placed on the fourth finger of the bride's right hand. She may change the ring to the fourth finger of her left hand after the ceremony. The bride may give the groom a ring if she desires.

The music you select must be agreed upon by the hazan (cantor) of the congregation. Where there is no hazan, the rabbi must be consulted.

Two male witnesses are required at all Jewish weddings and in most synagogues all men are required to cover their heads. Most women comply to show respect and, in deference to the same tradition, the bride wears a veil.

In Jewish tradition, the bride's family will be seated on the right side of the hall or temple, the groom's family will be seated on the left before any other guests are shown to their places.

Any of the above details may vary considerably according to denominations, so be certain to check every detail with your rabbi.

Before remarrying, Orthodox Jews must obtain a "Get," which is a religious sanction of divorce. Without it a remarriage cannot take place. The "Get" is given by the husband to the wife; a wife may not divorce her husband. For Conservative Jews, a statement in their ketubbah (marriage contract) allows both husband and wife to end their marriage. Reformed Jews are not under any jurisdiction from their rabbi. They believe that marriage and divorce are authorized by the state and not by religious disciplines.

CHURCH OF JESUS CHRIST OF LATTER-DAY SAINTS (LDS / MORMON)

The Church of Jesus Christ of Latter-day Saints recognizes two kinds of marriages. The first is for the faithful who are deemed fit for a religious marriage by a member of the Holy Priesthood. The second marriage is a civil ceremony.

To be allowed to be married inside an LDS temple, you must both have been baptized in the church. The groom must be an elder in the Melchizedek Priesthood and both of you together must receive a temple recommend from your bishop (who is the immediate church official).

The wedding takes place in a temple of the church where the bride and groom are sealed together for "time and all eternity" (in place of "until death do you part") in the eyes of God. Future children are sealed to you both at this time for life in the hereafter.

Both the bride and groom must wear all white during the ceremony. The bride's dress must have sleeves and must be modest in nature. The bride should not wear a veil, should not have a train on her dress, and is not allowed to have flowers inside of the temple.

The ceremony is performed by a temple official. You may request someone special if you know someone who meets the qualifications. Only persons having temple recommends may attend the ceremony. Those who do not have a recommend may wait in a waiting room inside the temple which allows them to be closer to the couple.

The actual ceremony is similar to a civil ceremony but the words spoken immediately before the ceremony are based on religious beliefs and are left to the discretion of the religious official.

Witnesses sign the wedding certificate and after the ceremony the attending wedding party is greeted by friends and relatives.

The couple then returns to the temple grounds where others are waiting to greet them and pictures are taken. The couple, accompanied by family and friends, will then usually attend a breakfast or luncheon which is followed in the evening by a reception.

In order to be married in the temple for a second time, a temple divorce must be granted.

A Mormon couple who is not married in the temple is married in a civil ceremony by a church or local official. They can later be married in the temple if they meet the requirements to receive a temple recommend.

RELIGIOUS SOCIETY OF FRIENDS (QUAKERS)

A Quaker wedding requires prior approval from the monthly meeting of the Religious Society of Friends. This process may take up to three months.

The wedding ceremony itself usually takes place during a meeting of worship where those in attendance meditate quietly. The bridal couple enters the meeting together and joins the Circle of Friends already seated. A traditional procession is an option if the bride wishes it. The bridal party then take seats on benches facing the meeting.

After the traditional Quaker silence, the bride and groom rise, join hands, and say their vows. The groom speaks his promises first, then the bride. A third person pronounces them married, for the Friends believe that only God can create such a union.

The marriage certificate is brought to the couple to sign after they have shared their vows. The certificate is then read aloud by a member of the meeting and signed by guests before departing, which is a custom couples in the Quaker faith treasure throughout their married life. The meeting may continue until the bride and groom feel ready to leave.

Additional details of the Quaker wedding are worked out in advance between the couple and an appointed group of meeting members. Couples today may choose to design almost any kind of personalized service they desire. The wedding remains a simple one, however, in keeping with the Quaker tradition.

In a traditional Quaker wedding, neither a bridal party nor the exchanging of rings is necessary and the bride is not given away.

CHRISTIAN SCIENCE CHURCH

Readers of the Christian Science faith are not ordained and may not perform marriages. When members of the faith marry, the ceremony may be performed by any minister ordained in another denomination or by the proper legal authority.

BUDDHIST

There are three denominations of the Buddhist religion: (1) Zen, (2) Jodo Shinshu, and (3) Nishi-ren. Each denomination has its own way of officiating wedding ceremonies.

Jodo Shinshu sect's wedding ceremony is patterned after the Protestant ceremony. It does not stress meditation like the Zen sect.

The traditional ceremony is as follows:
1. Ringing of the temple bell (outside)
2. Minister enters
3. Ushers escort grandparents and parents
4. Ushers light candles
5. Wedding music begins playing
6. Groom and his attendants enter
7. Wedding march begins
8. Bridal party enters
9. Your father presents you to the groom
10. Best man and maid-of-honor present rings to the minister
11. Minister asks your names
12. Recite Three Treasures
13. Recite Nembutsu
14. Minister chants Sutra
15. Minister chants Three Treasures
16. Minister reads wedding text
17. Consent of vows
18. Exchange of rings
19. Minister presents marriage license to groom
20. Minister recites the Buddhist "ojuzu" (rosary) to you and the groom

21. You both offer incense
22. Message by the minister
23. Wedding embrace
24. Minister and wedding party to gassho and bow together
25. Minister introduces the newlyweds
26. Recessional
27. Receiving line in temple entrance.

ISLAM / MUSLIM

It is forbidden for a Muslim woman to marry a non-Muslim man. A Muslim man, however, may marry a non-Muslim woman.

For the ceremony:
1. Witnesses, who need to be Muslim (unless you are not), and guests are seated as the bride and groom stand facing each other and holding hands.
2. The officiant offers a prayer.
3. You make a statement of intention and promise to follow the terms of the marital agreement.
4. The groom does the same.
5. You pledge your obedience and faithfulness to the groom.
6. The groom pledges his faithfulness and helpfulness to you.
7. Officiant offers final prayer and wishes.

ECUMENICAL

An ecumenical or interfaith ceremony is a symbolic demonstration of your determination to let your differences enrich each others lives. This ceremony is capable of setting a positive tone of cooperation, compromise, and understanding.

Members of two similar faiths would only have slight adjustments to make in their wedding ceremonies, but a marriage between a Christian and a Buddhist would require tremendous adaptation on both sides. The policy among interfaith marriages, sometimes known as ecumenical services among Christian groups, varies among denominations and religions. Some, such as Orthodox Jews, will not allow them under any circumstances. Churches that do allow interfaith ceremonies will often cooperate by allowing both church officiants to take part equally, and to incorporate the traditions of both faiths in the service. In some instances, however, you may request the ceremony to be performed almost entirely by one official with the other giving a short blessing at the end. The location of the marriage will depend on the denominations involved.

It is imperative that the church officiants communicate with one another early in the process. Usually, the person of the faith where the wedding is to be held will lead the planning process.

NONDENOMINATIONAL CEREMONIES

If you would like a church wedding, but do not agree with the religious beliefs of any specific faith, you may choose a nondenominational church such as Unitarian, which replaces creeds and laws with a philosophy of spiritual belief, for your ceremony.

Your ceremony can reflect whatever doctrine and personal religious feelings you wish to share and express. You can write your own or ask the minister for suggestions.

You only grow by coming to the end of something and by beginning something else.

John Irving

Choosing the Church Officiant

If you have belonged to the same faith and worshiped in the same place for an extended period, then choosing the person to perform the ceremony will be easy. For couples who have moved, been inactive in their faith, or who have no specified religious affiliation, this choice can be extremely difficult.

It is important that the two of you discuss every aspect of your religious feelings. Questions, concerns, and beliefs ranging from who will marry you to how you will raise your children, need to be discussed in detail.

Decide on what type of ceremony, who will perform the ceremony, and where you wish to have it held. Contact and meet with the official or officials you wish to have perform the ceremony as soon as possible. Have a list of questions and requests so that nothing will be forgotten and there will be no surprises. Discuss the ceremony, music, prayers, scriptures, vows and so on. Be certain to take care of any misunderstandings, misconceptions, and uncertainties before the wedding. Do not wait until the ceremony has begun or the wedding is over to voice an opinion or grievance.

Church Officiant Checklist

Officiant_____

Address_____

Phone_____

Fee_____

First Meeting
Date_____

Place_____

Time_____

Attendees_____

Second Meeting
Date_____

Place_____

Time_____

Attendees_____

Clergy Member Requirements_____

_____

_____

Date Completed_____

Church/Temple Requirements_____

_____

Church/Temple Fees_____

Date Completed_____

Bride and Groom's Special Requirements

_____

_____

_____

_____

Date Completed_____

Other Fees_____

Person in Charge of Giving Fees_____

_____

Rehearsal
Date_____

Place_____

Time_____

Ceremony Styles

Choose the style of ceremony that reflects the feelings, desires, and beliefs of both you and the groom. If that is a traditional religious ceremony, then the circumstances are dictated by the officiant, but if it is any variation on this theme, the two of you should express your desires and make certain they are incorporated into the entire wedding plan.

Formal: Steeped in tradition and laced with all of the pageantry and finery the occasion has to offer is the formal wedding. The ceremony is eloquent and religious, the wedding party is extensive, the gowns are grand, the men are dressed in tails, there are limousines to deliver the bride and her father to the church and to drive off with the groom and his newly beloved, and the reception that follows is truly an event to remember.

Semiformal: Most formal wedding procedures also apply to the smaller, semiformal wedding; they are simply done on a less lavish scale. You will have fewer guests, fewer attendants, and probably will not wear a dress with a train.

	Very Formal	Formal	Semiformal	Informal
Style	Traditional, elaborate	More relaxed, most popular	Between formal / informal	Catch-all, anything that you want
Ceremony	Church, temple synagogue, ballroom	Church, temple ballroom, country club	Anywhere proper	Anywhere desired
Reception	Large, lavish dinner and music	Dinner and music	Usually includes meal, maybe music	Small and simple
Guest List	Over 200 guests	Over 100 guests	Usually less than 100	Seldom more than 50
Bride	Elegant long dress, long veil/ sleeves, gloves, and train	Long dress, any sleeve length, short train, veil	Morning wedding-knee length; Evening wedding-floor length veil/hat/wreath	Dress / suit or casual clothing
Males	Cutaway, long jacket or stroller for day; tailcoat for night	Cutaway, stroller or tuxedo for day; tuxedo for night	Stroller, tuxedo dinner jacket for day; tuxedo, dinner jacket, suit or blazer for evening	Business suit, blazer
Female Attendants	6 - 8 attendants, long dress	2 - 6 attendants, long dress	1 - 3 attendants, dress based on length, style of bride	One attendant, dress or suit or casual

Informal: An intimate, informal wedding may be held anywhere from a small chapel to your home. Guests are welcomed and directed by a member of the wedding party who is familiar with almost everyone who is invited. You and the groom will probably mingle before the ceremony. At ceremony time, the two of you, your maid-of-honor and the best man take your places before the ceremony officiant. After the ceremony and the traditional kiss, the two of you simply turn to receive congratulations from the guests.

Religious: Personal preference, and the religious beliefs of you and your fiancé, will determine the type of religious wedding ceremony that you will have. If you are of one faith, the decision is easy. If you are of different denominations, you may agree on one ceremony, try to combine ideas from both, or write your own. The important thing is that you discuss the matter with each other and your clergy, and that each of you is in agreement with the final decision.

Each denomination will have different requirements and procedures and allowances for personal requests. Plans must be made for both of you to meet with the church officiant and then the three of you will decide on all aspects of the ceremony. Premarriage counseling is required by most religions.

Ecumenical (Interfaith): Each church may have different requirements and procedures in an interfaith ceremony so it is important to discuss the requirements with the officiant of both churches. The ceremonies are usually held on neutral grounds but in certain circumstances clergy members will allow interfaith weddings to take place in one or the other church. Usually a clergyman from both churches officiates during the ceremony. You will both have to meet with both clergymen at the same time to discuss the ceremony procedures and guidelines.

Nondenominational: This ceremony is usually similar to the traditional Protestant ceremony and possesses the flexibility for you to write part of your own vows. Its purpose is to allow you to be married with a spiritual essence without the structure and restrictions of established traditional religions. The ceremony can be offered by the Unitarian church or other nondenominational groups.

Civil: Most civil marriages are performed in a courthouse, a judge's chambers, the home of the justice of the peace, or at city hall. They are quiet, intimate, fast, easy, economical, and require only a marriage license. They can be performed by a variety of officials, for instance; a judge, your town's mayor, a justice of the peace, or a county clerk. Laws on who can marry you vary from county to county, so be certain to check with your marriage license bureau to find out what your state specifies.

The usual guidelines for an informal wedding apply with only you, the groom, and two witnesses attending.

If you are having a large civil ceremony performed at home or in a public facility like a country club or hotel, the procedures are the same as for a religious ceremony.

Traditional: The traditional wedding usually takes place in a church or temple and is performed by a clergy member of a religious faith. There are many variations based on the traditions and restrictions placed by the clergy member and the religion. Check individual types of ceremonies beginning on page 9 for more details.

Nontraditional: Some couples think the taking of vows in a church or hotel with any type of tradition attached is entirely too main stream for their wants or needs. They prefer an event that is associated with what they love to do together the most; those who love to ski can be married on the slopes, scuba-divers can be married under water, or if your husband-to-be is an avid baseball player, you could be married on home plate. Whatever it is that you want is exactly the way the ceremony should be handled.

If you prefer a nontraditional wedding, but do not care to go to the extremes of being married underwater, then a wedding that is considered contemporary in nature may take place in a giant lodge in the middle of the redwoods, at a historical site, or overlooking the ocean. Home garden weddings or resort weddings are also considered nontraditional but are becoming extremely popular in today's society.

*A life without love
is like a year without summer.*

Swedish

Older Bride: If you are an older bride for whom this is a first wedding, choose whatever traditions or fashions you desire. Any custom, any tradition, or any wording for the wedding vows is suitable and permissible for brides of any age. This is your day and it should be exactly as you want it to be.

Reaffirming Vows: If you eloped or had a very small wedding and now regret it, reaffirm your vows with all of the wedding frills. It is never too late to reaffirm your vows to one another and a new tradition of doing it with all of the celebrating that is traditionally associated with a first wedding is beginning to emerge.

Or, if you had a very large wedding the first time and this time want a quiet private ceremony shared only by the two of you, then this too is acceptable.

Second Marriages: This will be a special celebration of new hope, with a unique, wiser understanding of the commitment involved. People who have been married before tend to make their second wedding smaller and very personal. If, however, you or your groom want a more traditional wedding, then you should have one.

The second marriage can be anything the two of you want it to be. It can involve many of the traditions that are part of any bride's first wedding or you may want to do everything your own way. You may choose to have a small intimate wedding and a very large reception/ party to celebrate afterwards. If your plans include procedures that you feel certain family members or friends may disagree with, (like your wearing a long white wedding dress) then simply inform them of your plans ahead of time.

If either of you have children, you will want to have them participate in the ceremony and celebration. (See page 51 for involving children from a previous marriage.) You will want to inform the ex-spouse of the plans before putting the children in an uncomfortable situation. If you have remained close to your former in-laws, you may want to invite them as well. But you are not obligated to do so, nor are they expected to attend. An ex-spouse is rarely invited to the wedding, but that decision is also up to you and your fiancé.

If you want your second marriage to be a religious ceremony, most religious denominations allow for remarriage in certain situations. It is up to you and your fiancé to contact the church official of your choice and discuss the requirements of your individual faith.

Military Ceremony: The term "military ceremony" is a misnomer. A military wedding ceremony procedure does not actually exist. The ceremony is performed by the clergy member of your choice in the chapel on base. The military chaplain can perform the ceremony in uniform or religious attire. Outside the church, after the ceremony, the ushers (in uniform) face each other and arch their sabers (Army) or draw their swords (Navy). The bride and groom march under the arch as you leave the church and then kiss at the end. Civilian attendants do not take part in this ceremony, although they may line up with the officers. Enlisted personnel in the wedding party stand at attention.

Only commissioned officers may have the sword ceremony. A groom in any branch of military service, whether an officer or not, may be married in uniform, but swords and sabers are carried only by officers in full dress uniform. Traditionally, your father is the only man in the procession in civilian clothes, unless he is in the military as well. However, if you prefer, civilian tuxedos and gowns are allowed. If the groom lives on the military post, all officers and their wives should be invited to the ceremony and reception. If your fiancé lives off base, invite only the commanding officer, post commander, and their wives. Rank should be carefully observed when seating guests; high ranking officers should receive seats of honor.

Invitations and announcements differ only in that the groom's rank and service are indicated. You and the groom may use either the Officer's Club or other facilities on the base for the reception. Wedding decorations include the American flag and the standards of the groom's unit, in addition to the flowers. If your groom is in uniform, it is customary for him to cut the wedding cake with his sword or saber.

Double Wedding: Double weddings offer twice of everything while cutting down on the expense for both couples. Requirements for a double wedding ceremony are the same as for a single wedding. Both couples decide together on the type of ceremony and consult a clergy member about the requirements.

Most often a double wedding is a formal affair. The two brides should wear similar gowns; one bride should not stand out more than the other. The attendants can wear different colors and styles as long as they complement each other. The groom and the ushers can wear either the same colors or coordinating colors to match their wedding party.

Both brides and grooms select their own wedding attendants. Often the bride and groom will be the maid-of-honor and best man in each other's weddings.

Invitations are usually issued jointly, but if the brides are not sisters, separate invitations may be sent.

During the processional and recessional, traditionally, the older of the two brides goes first. If there are two aisles, both brides can walk down simultaneously. With a single aisle, the two grooms walk in together behind the clergy member and take their places side-by-side, each with his own best man behind him, the future husband of the first bride standing nearer the aisle. Both sets of ushers, paired by height, head the procession. The bridesmaids, honor attendant, and flower girl of the first bride come next, followed by the bride on her father's arm. The second set of attendants and the second bride follow in similar fashion.

If the two brides are sisters, there are a myriad of possibilities of who can give the brides away. The father and a brother, the father and the mother, or the father can escort both brides together.

On reaching the head of the aisle, the attendants usually separate so that those of the first bride are on the left, those of the second bride on the right. The two couples stand side by side in front of the wedding official, the first bride on the left. The ceremony may be divided into two sections, with each couple completing each section in turn: first one couple speaks their vows, then the other. However, the final blessing may be given to both at the same time. The recession is led by the two couples, one preceding the other, followed by the two sets of honor attendants, the bridesmaids and ushers in pairs.

If the brides are related, only one receiving line is necessary. If the brides are not related, having two separate lines is more appropriate.

The Weekend Wedding: If you are a couple who have friends and family who live in different parts of the country and it is difficult for you to see them, you might want to plan a weekend wedding. Your rehearsal might take place earlier in the week, leaving Friday evening clear for a dinner to greet your arriving guests. Your ceremony may take place any time during the weekend with you and your groom enjoying the weekend with your guests and then leaving on your honeymoon.

The weekend wedding may be held in a country inn, a hotel at the beach, a mountain resort or a favorite vacation spot. A typical weekend schedule includes a Friday night get-together; small-group breakfasts and activities Saturday morning; the wedding Saturday afternoon or early evening; a wedding night reception; and a Sunday good-bye brunch.

This type of wedding is more expensive for all involved so you must be prepared for additional costs for yourselves and your guests. You might want to offer guests a special welcome with baskets filled with goodies in their rooms. Do not forget to thank them for coming so far to participate in your wedding celebration. Traditionally, you make all of the reservations for out-of-town relatives and friends, but they pay their own hotel bills; this should be worked out in advance so there are no misunderstandings. The bride pays the hotel bills of her out-of-town attendants, the groom's family pays for the hotel bills of the out-of-town groomsmen. Everyone pays for his/her own transportation.

Elopement: The ceremony for an elopement is usually performed at a rectory, city hall, small church, or designated wedding chapel. The ceremony is usually simple and fast with only the bride, groom, officiating officer, and two witnesses present.

The goal in marriage is not to think alike but to think together.

Carolyn Heilbrun

Ceremony Checklist

Officiant_____

Phone_____

Officiant Fee_____

Location of Ceremony_____

Address_____

Phone_____

Person in Charge of Location_____

Fee_____

Transportation_____

Person in Charge of Transportation_____

Arrival Time_____

Where to Dress_____

Time to Begin_____

Opening Words by_____

Readings By_____

Prayers Given By_____

Changes in Marriage Vows_____

Music_____

_____

Organist_____

Soloists_____

Musicians_____

Closing Words by_____

Time to End_____

Rehearsal Date_____

Time_____

Coordinator for Rehearsal_____

Phone_____

Guest Book/Pen_____

Person in Charge_____

Wedding Programs_____

Person in Charge_____

Reserved Seating/Bride
Names/Pew 1_____

Names/Pew 2_____

Names/Pew 3_____

Usher in Charge_____

Reserved Seating/Groom

Names/Pew 1_____

Names/Pew 2_____

Names/Pew 3_____

Usher in Charge_____

Person to Accept Gifts_____

Phone_____

Servers_____

Person in Charge_____

Phone_____

Rice/Flower Petals_____

Person in Charge_____

Janitor_____

Janitor Fees_____

Parking Availability_____

Parking Attendants_____

_____

_____

_____

Photo Session

Photographer_____

Location_____

Time_____

Marriage License_____

Important Phone Numbers

Bride's_____

Bride's Parents_____

Groom_____

Groom's Parents_____

Wedding Coordinator_____

Notes

Symbolic Ceremonies

Wedding Ring Ceremony: The wedding ring's circular shape symbolizes eternal love. This part of the ceremony is traditional in most weddings and mandatory in the Jewish wedding.

The best man or ring bearer usually carries both rings and hands them to the officiant during the ceremony. The officiant briefly describes the history behind the custom and passes the rings to the bride and groom. The groom places the ring on the bride's left hand, fourth finger. Then the bride places the groom's ring on his left hand, fourth finger.

Wine Ceremony: This ceremony is part of many Christian wedding ceremonies. A glass of wine is shared to symbolize sharing your lives together with God. The wine service is usually part of a religious wedding ceremony but at civil ceremonies may be celebrated when the cake is cut at the reception.

Lighting Of The Unity Candle: This candle service symbolizing family unity has become increasingly popular in recent decades. The bright flame of love is kindled with the light of life of the two families. Three candles are lit in turn: the bride's parents light the right, the groom's parents light the left, and the couple themselves set the center taper aflame with the light from those two.

A Candlelight Ceremony: When the wedding is to take place in the evening and the ceremony site is a dark one, a candlelight ceremony can be very beautiful. You must, however, meet with whomever is in charge of the building to discuss the restrictions on the number and placement of the candles.

Placement of the candles to shine throughout the church should be carefully considered–they need to be kept out of doorways and drafts. There may need to be special arrangements made so the officiant has extra light at the altar. You will need to decide if you want them on stands and if the stands should be decorated.

Designated assistants, whether ushers, friends, or church choir boys proceed slowly up the aisle, lighting the candles shortly before the procession is to begin. Your attendants will then make their way down the aisle, to a very slow wedding march holding lighted candles. (The florist can provide holders that are easy to grip and will catch the wax.)

Candles may also take on a symbolic meaning during the ceremony. Two candles might flicker during the service–one on the bride's side of the church, the other on the groom's, with a taller candle in the center– which remains unlit until the officiant announces you are husband and wife. Each of you then take your candle and the two of you light the candle in the middle, indicating the joining of the two individuals and/or families.

Once the recessional has occurred and before the ushers direct the guests to depart, those appointed make their way back toward the altar, snuffing the candles row by row as the music continues to play. Or, if you choose the guests may walk out under candlelight.

Other Symbolic Ceremonies
1. Have the church bells rung immediately after you say your vows.
2. As you walk up the aisle, take a single flower from your bouquet and hand it to your mother and then cross the aisle and do the same for his mother.
3. As you and the groom begin the recessional, stop and give each father a kiss and each mother a flower and a kiss.
4. For a small wedding, have the ushers give each female guest a single flower as she arrives.
5. As you leave the church for the reception, have helium balloons sent skyward signaling your unending hope for the future.

The greatest joys are celebrations of the heart.

Flavia

Special Circumstances Related to the Ceremony

The traditional family is no longer the norm in American culture. In today's society, the many variations need to be addressed. The following suggestions cover some of the special circumstances that may apply to your wedding. Use your best judgment and heed the advice of professionals when making decisions about handling these special circumstances. Remember, your wedding will raise many emotions, both good and bad, so be prepared to deal with them. Discuss your options with your fiancé. Consider all of the variables and then make a decision. Let all of those concerned know what the two of you have decided so there will be no surprises for them or you on your wedding day.

Escort And Who Gives You Away: If your parents are divorced and neither parent has remarried, your father will escort you unless you feel it would be more appropriate for someone else to do so. If your mother has recently remarried, traditionally your father should still escort you because your stepfather did not raise you.

If your parents divorced when you were a young child and your mother and stepfather raised you, you may choose to have your stepfather escort you down the aisle. If both stepfather and father raised you, consider all possible options: both could walk you down the aisle, one on each side of you; one could walk you down the aisle and one could stand at the altar to give you away; you could have your mother walk you down the aisle; or you could ask them what their thoughts are on the matter before you make your decision. Whichever you choose, be certain to tell the involved parties as soon as possible in order to alleviate as many hurt feelings as possible.

If Your Father Has Passed Away: Planning your wedding will bring forth feelings of sadness and loss if your father is deceased. In such cases, however, you may choose to have your mother walk you down the aisle, an older or younger brother, a stepfather, uncle, godfather, future father-in-law, or very close friend. Choose someone to whom you feel attached; it is a special honor for both of you.

Children From First Marriages: It is important that children from previous marriages do not feel left out of any of the plans for your wedding or for your future. This is especially true of younger children. Make the children an integral part of your plans. If they are only children, make them your maid-of-honor or best man, or attendants and ushers, if there are more. If they are very young, they can be flower girls or ring bearers. Whatever their role, be certain to make each child feel very important and give each child a special gift to commemorate the day.

In some second marriages, the children are actually included in the ceremony. After the bride and groom have been united, the children are officially united as well. After all, a marriage is a creation of an entirely new family and the growth and dynamics of this new family can start on a wonderfully positive note by including everyone in the celebration.

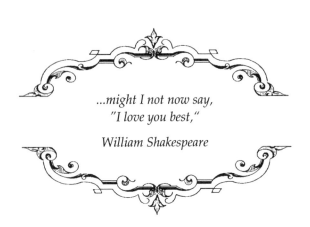

...might I not now say, "I love you best,"

William Shakespeare

Ceremony Vows

Wedding vows are public and intimate pronouncements where the two of you make promises to each other in front of your guests. They can be a beautifully sentimental combination of your family tradition and your contemporary beliefs.

If you have decided on a religious ceremony, you will need to talk to your clergy member about the ceremony and vows. Ask him to give you a copy of the traditional vows to review so that you can decide beforehand if they are representative of your feelings and beliefs.

Discuss the realm of possibilities with your clergy member. He or she is possibly your best source of ideas and references. Browse through books at the church, library or bookstore. Consider poetry, literature or original work as possible inclusions.

Your vows and ceremony should represent the way you feel about each other and what your marriage means to the two of you. You may even ask family and friends to contribute to your vows and/or to participate during the ceremony.

Making Your Wedding Vows Special

If you choose to write your own wedding vows or to personalize existing vows, you may want to incorporate one or more of the following ideas:

1. Personalize existing vows:

a. You may want to reword certain phrases in existing vows to update them. For example, "to love and obey" could be read "to love and cherish."

b. You may want to delete certain phrases altogether.

c. You may want certain family members to participate in the ceremony by adding readings to existing vows. For example, your father may want to write or read a short passage, on behalf of his family, expressing happiness for the new couple-to-be. Children from a previous marriage may want to read a passage about new families.

d. You may want to incorporate a public expression of love into the ceremony to honor a parent or close family member by reading a short verse or asking them to do so.

e. You may want to incorporate special music into different parts of the ceremony to emphasize a particular segment of the sermon.

f. You may choose to recite your vows from memory.

g. While not part of the vows themselves, a personal note is added when the officiant closes the ceremony by introducing you and the groom as "Mr. and Mrs. —."

2. *Write your own vows:*
   a. Acknowledge wedding participants, family, and guests.
   b. Describe the ideals of the marriage you are about to enter into.
   c. Describe the important facets of your relationship.
   d. Describe the direction and hope for your future–relationship, parenthood, friendship, companionship.
   e. Describe your commitment to one another now and forever.
   f. If applicable, you may want to discuss certain religious aspects of your union.
   g. Restate your love for one another.

3. *References for writing your vows:*
   a. Simply write down your own thoughts and feelings.
   b. Refer to scriptures in the Bible indexed under love, marriage, family, and togetherness.
   c. Say a personal prayer that you learned as a child or have learned lately.
   d. Children's stories such as *The Little Prince* and *The Velveteen Rabbit* have wonderful sections that could be retold.
   e. Writings from authors such as Kahlil Gibran, poetry by anyone or such notables as Elizabeth Barret Browning, Shakespeare, Carl Sandburg, and E.E. Cummings can be used.
   f. Take lines from pieces of music.

4. Rules of etiquette when personalizing your vows:

    a. The entire ceremony should not extend past one hour.

    b. If you ask anyone else to participate, make certain they feel comfortable doing so.

    c. Make certain you have gone over all changes, additions, and deletions with the ceremony officiant, religious or otherwise.

Notes

Ceremony Music

Shakespeare said it best: "If music be the food of love, play on." The music you and/or the groom select for your ceremony is a very important part of your wedding. Before making your final musical selections, it is necessary to check with the church officiant you have selected. There may be rules governing musical pieces during the ceremony that you are unaware of.

If you do not personally know of anyone to play or sing at your wedding, you may want to try one of the following :

1. Ask friends or family members.
2. Scout college musical performances.
3. Ask a professional referral service, musicians union, or other established performance groups.
4. Attend local nightclubs and listen to the groups performing.

Below is a list of suggestions for selecting your wedding music:

1. Meet with the organist before you begin selecting your music; he/she may be well qualified in helping you. But remember, if he/she is accustomed to traditional wedding pieces and marches, you should not feel hesitant about insisting on more updated or personal selections. Keep in mind the church guidelines you have discussed with your officiant.

2. Meet with the soloists–vocal or instrumental–and discuss the same topics you discussed with the organist. Some soloists perform professionally and may also have suggestions as to musical selections that work particularly well. A professional may ask to use his/her own accompanist. If you are asking a friend or family member to perform during the ceremony, make certain they feel comfortable doing so. If they are inexperienced, give them the music you have selected and allow enough time for them to practice.

3. Make the final decisions on musical selections and who will perform them as soon as possible. You may want to have alternate selections in case you have trouble finding the music or the musician you have chosen feels incapable of playing that particular selection.

4. The musical participants should also be informed as to what they should wear to the ceremony as soon as possible. Discuss all of the options and be considerate of the wardrobe they have. If you feel strongly that they wear something specific or unusual, you may be required to pay for the purchase or rental of the garments.

5. Music is a service rendered just as are the wedding consultant and the photographer. Be certain to discuss the organist's and musicians' fees and make arrangements for them to be paid at the rehearsal dinner. If a friend or family member is participating and you feel a cash payment is inappropriate, then give a nice gift or memento of the day. If the participant is required to travel long distances and stay in outside accommodations, you may offer to pay for the room in exchange for his/her agreeing to perform.

6. If it is necessary to order music, be certain you are ordering the correct music with the correct accompaniment information. Have in writing the exact title, the composer and/or arranger, the voice range, and the type of accompaniment needed. If possible, know the publisher. In many cases, the musician may already have the music or want to order his/her own. Some musicians may request a tape of the way you like the music played, so that they can perform it to your interpretation and not their own.

7. Be certain to obtain enough copies of each piece of music for each musician.

8. Be certain to receive a list of and order all additional equipment that the musicians will need. If they require special seats, stands, or microphones, you will need to order these before hand so that they will be available and in working order for the rehearsal and the ceremony.

9. The soloists–vocal and instrumental– should rehearse with the organist/accompanist before the wedding is to take place.

10. All musical participants should attend the rehearsal dinner and be prepared to perform their selections. You should have a schedule of events that you can give to each one so he/she will have a copy of what is expected when. They should also bring with them the clothing they will be wearing during the ceremony so that you can be certain all is as expected.

11. At the rehearsal, double check the musicians' equipment needs.

Prelude music can begin forty-five minutes to one hour before the ceremony. In a church wedding, these pieces are usually classical organ music, although small ensembles of other instruments, such as a pianist, a guitar player, or a harpist, are sometimes used.

If you are having a soloist, the time immediately before the processional is an excellent time for a song. Other songs may fit nicely after the sermon, before the vows, or placed intermittently throughout the ceremony.

The wedding march may be the traditional "Here Comes The Bride" or a personal selection that is more appropriate for you and the groom. It should be joyful and quietly majestic. The recessional selection should be a different piece from the processional and should have a slightly faster tempo.

Notes for Possible Music Selections

Checklist for Ceremony Music

Prelude
Performer_____

Selection_____

Time to Begin_____

First Solo
Performer_____

Selection_____

Time to Begin_____

Processional
Performer_____

Selection_____

Time to Begin_____

Wedding March
Performer_____

Selection_____

Time to Begin_____

Second Solo
Performer_____

Selection_____

Time to Begin_____

Additional Solos
Performer(s)_____

_____

_____

Selection(s)_____

_____

_____

Time(s) to Begin_____

Recessional
Performer_____

Selection_____

Time to Begin_____

Postlude
Performer_____

Selection_____

Time to Begin_____

Time to End_____

Music Participant's Personal Information

Organist

Name_____

Address_____

Phone_____

Fee_____

Attire_____

Musicians

Name_____

Address_____

Phone _____

Fee_____

Attire_____

Soloists

Name_____

Address_____

Phone _____

Fee_____

Attire_____

Name_____

Address_____

Phone _____

Fee_____

Attire_____

Notes

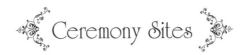

Ceremony Sites

Once you have decided on your wedding style, you will need to select the location. Local visitors bureaus may have a guide to local facilities that are available for weddings and receptions. Your local chamber of commerce or historical society office may have additional leads. Local parks departments will know the availability, requirements, and restrictions for public sites often used for wedding ceremonies.

Begin your search for a ceremony site as soon as you have selected the date for your wedding. Prime dates can book up to a year in advance. Popular months for weddings vary by regions: December in the South, Valentine's Day everywhere, and weekends in June are almost impossible to book on either coast. Be aware that religious restrictions may rule out certain days or times of the year. For example, Catholics and Greek Orthodox avoid marrying during Lent in March and Jews do not have weddings during the High Holy Days (usually in September and October).

If you plan your ceremony to take place in a location other than a church, keep in mind the preparations you may have to orchestrate. Consider all of the details, including such items as how accessible the site is, what facilities exist for guest parking and seating, and what equipment is available. If it is outdoors, remember to select a quiet spot that is away from the traffic. It would be wise to select an alternate location in case the weather is bad.

CHURCH / TEMPLE / SYNAGOGUE

If you have chosen a traditional religious wedding and you both belong to the same church, your decision is easy. On the other hand, if different affiliations need to be considered, you will need to make certain that both of you are happy with the final decision of where and how the ceremony should be conducted. If neither of you belongs to a religious denomination, find a place that you like, talk to the clergyman and discuss policies for marrying nonmembers.

You will need to make certain that the religious site and the officiant you have selected are available on the day and time required. Many facilities have literature listing their policies in regard to all aspects of weddings, such as music, flash photography, videos, rice, candlelight, and so on.

RECTORY

The rectory wedding ceremony is performed for those who prefer a religious, private ceremony. Some brides dislike being the center of attention, even at their own wedding. In these circumstances the rectory wedding (or a small private ceremony held at a nonreligious site) is an acceptable alternative. These private ceremonies can be conducted for the bride and groom and whomever they wish to include. The requirements are the same as for weddings in a public setting. Request a meeting with your clergy member (or ceremony officiant) to discuss requirements and procedures.

HOTEL / CLUB / RESTAURANT

Consider all possibilities for the atmosphere, room size, and price range that suit your needs and wants best. There is often no charge for site rental if the establishment caters the reception–although this option is not always as cost-effective as it sounds. This choice is usually made if both the ceremony and reception are to occur in the same location.

CITY HALL / JUSTICE OF THE PEACE

Make an appointment to discuss details and fees. This type of wedding is always informal; flowers, guests, and other extras are kept to a minimum. However, do not hesitate to ask a friend to come and photograph the ceremony–it is still your wedding day regardless of how simple it is.

WEDDING CHAPEL

The wedding chapel is a commercial wedding site. Its sole purpose is to marry couples from any denomination. It can be as elaborate as the wedding chapel on the Queen

Mary or as simple as the wedding chapels in Las Vegas.

Some wedding chapels operate the same as any other wedding ceremony site. The site is rented for a fee and you provide everything else yourself, including clergy, flowers, and so on. Others have package deals that include all of the above for one fee.

Wedding chapels are predominately found in California, Nevada, and the Southwest. Most of these states have confidential marriage certificates and will also allow the couple to be married on the same day. Inquire ahead of time as to the specific requirements of the chapel you are selecting so there will be no delays when you arrive.

HOME CEREMONY

Traditionally your parents' home was the only choice, although now it has become acceptable for the home of a close friend or relative to provide the perfect setting for your wedding ceremony. You must remember, however, that to have a large wedding in a home is indeed entertaining on a grand scale and the preparation may be more than you anticipate. Organization and delegation of responsibilities are essential. Do consider hiring a wedding coordinator to handle all of the arrangements so that nothing will be overlooked. You can probably rent everything you need through a rental agency.

Your mother or a close friend usually greets guests at the door and directs them to the ceremony site. The groom's parents mingle with the guests until the ceremony is to begin. Formal seating is not required, but you may wish to provide chairs for the guests. The procession should be modified from the traditional one. At the end of the ceremony you and the groom will turn and greet your guests in a type of informal receiving line.

OUTDOORS

A large garden or park is a perfect place for an outdoor wedding that ranges from formal to informal. Procedures for an outdoor wedding are similar to those for any other wedding in a private location. The procedures for greeting, seating, and receiving congratulations from your guests are the same as for the home wedding.

If you are certain you desire an outdoor wedding but do not know the best place, try consulting the chamber of commerce, private clubs, historic sites, private estates, or parks departments. Contact the person in charge of the location and discuss all details with him/her. Sign a contract that specifies all aspects of renting or using the location: arrival times, departure times, equipment that can be used, clean-up responsibilities, parking facility use, and others. Make certain that you have obtained all permits and that you have arranged to pay all deposits and fees.

If possible, spend the same day of the week at the same hours the ceremony will be performed at your site to thoroughly familiarize yourself with the daily traffic. Be aware of the time of day and the temperature. You do not want to have guests in the hot sun or you and the groom staring into the afternoon sun.

Make a map and mail to guests so they will know how to get there. You will be wise to arrange for alternate sites in case of bad weather. You might even enclose a small card with the invitation, giving this kind of information: "In the event of inclement weather, the wedding will be held at ____." You may want to arrange for large party tents to ensure that the ceremony goes off no matter what.

ALTERNATIVE OPTIONS

You may choose to be married at a local historic mansion, famous garden, art gallery, or historical site. Some couples are wed on rented yachts, others in private rail cars. Perhaps the spot where he proposed, or a place special to the two of you, will be the place you select for the ceremony.

When families are scattered across the country, some couples are reviving the old-fashioned ethnic tradition of multiday celebrations. The families gather for a long weekend of parties and activities–the ceremony and reception are just part of the fun. Other couples celebrate in two or more locations with ceremonies and parties at both.

Ceremony Site Checklist

Type of Ceremony_____

Date_____

Time_____

Location_____

Address_____

Person in Charge_____

Phone Number_____

Clergy/Officiant_____

Phone Number_____

Minimum Guests_____

Maximum Guests_____

Length of Time Available_____

Earliest Arrival Time_____

Departure Time_____

Fees/Due Date_____

Floral Arrangements Setup Time_____

Details
Runner_____

Rice/Flower Throwing_____

Equipment/Costs
Wedding Altar_____

Wedding Arch_____

Guest Book Table_____

Aisle Stanchions_____

Chairs_____

Candelabras_____

Candles_____

Kneeling Bench_____

Rehearsal Time_____

Dressing Rooms_____

Number_____

Time Available_____

Photography Rules and Restrictions_____

_____

Photography Setup Time_____

Audio Equipment/Cost_____

Gift Table_____

Person in Charge of
Removal of Flowers to Reception Site

_____

Other_____

Coat/Hat Room Attendant_____

Fees Due/Date_____

Janitor_____

Fees for Janitor_____

Parking Availability_____

Parking Attendants_____

Notes

Ceremony Seating

There should be adequate seating for all invited guests to sit comfortably. If the ceremony site is too large with more seating than required, try to section off an area. This will prevent guests from being seated at random throughout the church.

Ushers should begin seating guests as soon as they arrive at the ceremony site. Eldest guests are seated first if a group of guests arrive at the same time. The usher offers the woman his right arm and escorts her down the aisle to the appropriate side. The bride's guests are seated on the left side and the groom's guests are seated on the right side (reversed for a Jewish ceremony). If a woman arrives with her husband, he follows behind the usher and his wife. If the guest is an elderly man, the usher offers his right arm to escort him to his seat.

If either you or the groom have significantly more guests than the other, use the traditional seating for the reserved pews only. Ushers can then seat all other guests on either side.

Reserved Section Seating: Mark the reserved pews with ribbons, flowers, or "Reserved" signs so guests will not sit in those sections. You may want to send reserved pew seating cards to appropriate guests with their invitations so they can hand it to the usher when they arrive.

The bride's parents sit in the first pews on the left side. Your grandparents, siblings, or children can also sit in the first pews. Special aunts and uncles can sit in the second and third rows. The groom's family is seated in the same manner but on the right side.

If either your parents or the groom's parents are divorced, the mother and her husband sit in the first pew and the father and his wife sit in the second pew (unless you feel it is appropriate to have both parents and spouses sit together).

It is important for you or the wedding coordinator to decide ahead of time whether the ushers or the florist are to set up the pew ribbons, if any are being used. If the ushers are to do so, assign two ushers to be responsible. They should also remove both ribbons and aisle carpet following the ceremony after the guests have gone.

To avoid congestion and confusion after the ceremony the ushers can signal guests to leave row by row, starting with the first row of reserved seats. The ushers untie the pew ribbons on each side simultaneously, one row at a time, and motion to guests with their arms to exit. Have the ushers practice so their timing is uniform. The guests leave in an organized fashion. This is a good system if you plan to have your receiving line outside of the church. All of the guests will be exiting slowly.

For smaller weddings, guests can exit on their own. After the recessional, the parents and relatives in the first pews exit, then all of the guests stand and leave using any aisle.

Reserved Section Checklist

First Pew
Bride's Section———————————————

———————————————————————

———————————————————————

———————————————————————

———————————————————————

Groom's Section———————————————

———————————————————————

———————————————————————

———————————————————————

———————————————————————

———————————————————————

Second Pew
Bride's Section_____

_____

_____

_____

Groom's Section_____

_____

_____

_____

Third Pew
Bride's Section_____

_____

_____

Groom's Section_____

_____

_____

Head usher responsible for reserved section
seating:
_____

Ceremony Programs

If you are going to have printed ceremony programs, you may want to include some of the following information. Programs are not only nice momentos, they are an unobtrusive answer to "who is who?"

Program Title: This section is generally positioned at the top of the inside left-hand page for programs with full cover designs and includes the following:

1. Descriptive phrase
2. Bride's name
3. Groom's name
4. Day and date
5. Time
6. Ceremony location
7. City and state

Some Suggestions for Descriptive Phrases Are:

THE WEDDING CEREMONY OF

THE SACRAMENT OF
HOLY MATRIMONY
UNITING

THE CELEBRATION AND BLESSING
OF THE MARRIAGE UNITING

THE MARRIAGE CELEBRATION OF

THE RELIGIOUS CEREMONY
UNITING IN MARRIAGE

Order of the Service: The order of the service outlines the individual segments: prelude, processional, solo, invocation, scripture reading, marriage ceremony, lighting of the unity candle, benediction, and recessional. Depending on the faith, the customs and the selected ritual, the terminology will vary. It is necessary to consult with your church officiant regarding the exact order of the service.

Other items you may wish to include are music titles with participants, book and poem titles with author and/or readers, scripture passages with readers, hymn titles with hymnal page numbers, words for short congregational prayers, and any special notations.

Participants: Participants can be grouped and sequenced using titled headers to separate the groupings, or everyone may be listed in a logical sequence under the single heading "Wedding Participants." Be consistent with respect to naming individuals. Names may be preceded with titles such as Mrs., Ms., or Miss and given names should be used, instead of nicknames.

Messages and Notations: This section can be positioned at the bottom of the inside right-hand page or on the program back, if it is blank. Short personal messages or expressions of thanks to the guests from the bride and groom are very appropriate and make for a lasting keepsake. As an alternative to the personal message, a special prayer, poem, or short quotation might express your feelings. Notations regarding the reception, the bride and groom's new home address or other information you wish to convey to the guests should be at the bottom of the page.

Marriage License

License: Call your county clerk's office about requirements and to see if it is necessary to set up an appointment for a marriage license. Most states require proof of citizenship, proof of age, state health certificate, and proof of divorce (if necessary). Gather these certificates together before you go to apply for the license. Most states require that the marriage license be applied for no more than thirty days prior to the wedding. If you are under eighteen, there may be additional requirements. There is often a fee for the license and you and your fiancé will probably be required to apply together.

Confidential Marriage License: A confidential marriage license is kept under seal by the state. Check to see if the requirements are the same to obtain this license. This license was adopted for couples who wanted to prevent their children from discovering their parent's marriage dates. Pregnant brides can get married to protect their children's legitimacy and inheritance without public record of the wedding date.

Marriage License Checklist

County Clerk _____

Address_____

Phone_____

Hours_____

Marriage License Fees_____

Waiting Period after Application_____

Marriage License Valid for_____

Appointment with County Clerk_____

Time_____

Date_____

Documents Required by County Clerk

Proof of Citizenship_____
(Driver's License)

Proof of Age_____
(Birth Certificate)

Proof of Divorce_____
(If applicable)

Letters of Consent_____
(If a Minor)

The Ceremony Rehearsal

Your wedding ceremony is one of the most important events the two of you will ever share. It will be steeped in tradition and laced with personal touches. To make certain your ceremony is everything you want it to be, you must be organized from the beginning and you must plan a rehearsal to give yourself and the entire wedding party a chance to practice each part, answer each question, and attend to last minute details.

Discuss all of your ceremony plans at a premarriage conference held with the officiant, the bride, the groom, and the wedding consultant, if appropriate. The time to discuss the details and ask any questions is at this meeting and not at the actual rehearsal when everyone else is present. If you take the time to go over your plans with parents, attendants, and then, finally, the clergy ahead of time, there will be no surprises or hurt feelings.

1. The presence of every member of the actual wedding party is of the utmost importance at the rehearsal. However, discourage wedding party spouses and friends from attending the actual rehearsal, and invite them to the rehearsal dinner or party afterwards. Include the bridal consultant, if one is being employed. It is a nice idea to invite out-of-town guests who have traveled a considerable distance to also attend the rehearsal dinner, but not the rehearsal. They have incurred much time and expense to be there, and this is a nice way of saying thank you.

2. It is a good idea to send out written invitations to those you want to be at the rehearsal ceremony and dinner. This reminds everyone where they are to be and when, and leaves no doubt in anyone's mind about whether attendance is required, what time their mates should arrive for the dinner, and how long the evening will be.

3. The wedding rehearsal should be scheduled to allow at least two hours. It should be scheduled shortly before the wedding and be conducted in the location where the ceremony is to be performed.

4. Traditionally, the rehearsal takes place the night before the wedding with a rehearsal dinner for participants following. However, it is appropriate to hold it up to five days before the festivities.

5. Take pictures at the rehearsal. These are memories that will last a lifetime, and, because you are so nervous or busy, you may not get to see everything that happens.

6. The organist and members of the church staff who are assisting with the ceremony must also be present at the rehearsal. These participants should be notified by the bride, the person placed in charge of the rehearsal or the church secretary.

7. Remind each participant to dress appropriately. The type of dinner or the church itself may impose restrictions on attire.

8. The bridal consultant should also be notified of the time and date of the rehearsal and should be present to offer needed services, but should in no way interfere with the conduct of the rehearsal.

9. For a religious ceremony, the clergyman will be the determining factor in certain aspects of the ceremony. He/she is the only one who can give instructions as to how the ceremony must be conducted, as he/she is the only one who knows and understands the rules by which he/she is governed.

10. For a civil ceremony, the bride and the groom (with the help of the wedding consultant, if one is being employed) can decide on the procedure of the ceremony. This is your day and you should be allowed to state how it will proceed. If, however, you are unsure as to what to do in exactly what order, the traditional guidelines outlined in this book will help in making your decisions.

11. The marriage service will not be read in full at the rehearsal, so go over any special requests or variations needed to understand the exact order of events and to outline the roles of the wedding party involved. All participants, whether taking pictures or performing a musical selection, should do an actual run through of their parts. Practice will help reinforce understanding of their roles so there will be no mistakes. You may want to be as detailed as bringing stand-in bouquets, the rings, the ring bearer's cushion, and other props, so that everyone can practice his/her part.

12. Practice passing the bouquet. After you reach the altar, your maid-of-honor will pass her bouquet to the next in line so she can adjust your gown and train. You can either pass her your bouquet now so your hands will be free during the ceremony or you can wait until the exchange of the ring(s) to give her your flowers. At the end of the ceremony, your maid-of-honor hands back your bouquet, adjusts your gown, and you begin the recessional.

13. Practice exchanging the rings. The best man or the ring bearer holds the rings during the ceremony. At the appropriate time, the best man produces the rings, either from his pocket or from the cushion, and hands them to the clergy member. The clergy member hands the bride's ring to the groom with his palms up. This will eliminate the possibility of the ring being dropped during the handing off. He does the same for the bride.

14. Make certain the photographer knows when it is and is not appropriate to take pictures during the ceremony. Also, arrange with him for the required pictures immediately before and after the ceremony. A very specific list may save confusion and disappointment.

15. Before the rehearsal is over, repeat all of the instructions, times, and places with each participant individually. Give each person a checklist. Let each person explain to you individually what his/her responsibilities are so there are no misunderstandings. Ask if there are any questions and answer them immediately.

16. The wedding coordinator should receive a copy of each checklist along with the ceremony and reception checklists. Give the coordinator a checklist with the wedding party's names, addresses, and all of the details about the services (florist, photographer, musicians, and so on). That way, if someone forgets a task, the coordinator can remind him/her or assist with other problems that might arise, such as the florist being late.

17. Have the officiant check the marriage license and make certain the witnesses have been notified and have given their consent to signing on your behalf.

18. A rehearsal for a ceremony of any size is reassuring for everyone involved, but some clergy members or civil officials do not schedule one for small ceremonies or those being held in public places. In that case, everyone should assemble a little early so brief instructions can be given in advance.

Ceremony Rehearsal Checklist

Date_____

Time_____

Location_____

Phone_____

Coordinator for Rehearsal_____

Phone_____

Invitations_____

Organist_____

Phone_____

Soloist_____

Phone_____

Other Musicians_____

Phone_____

Musical Selections_____

_____

_____

Checklists for Attendants_____

Wedding Ceremony and
Reception Checklist_____

Checklists for Parents_____

Checklists for Helpers_____

Coordinator's Checklist_____

Marriage License_____

Practice Bouquet _____

Wine Goblets, Wine, and Corkscrew
(for certain religious ceremonies)_____

_____

Fees for Clergy Member _____

Fees for Musicians_____

Fees for Site Rental_____

Other Fees_____

Gifts for Altar Boys_____

Gifts for Wedding Party_____

Camera and Film_____

Notes

The Rehearsal Dinner

The rehearsal dinner, traditionally held immediately after the rehearsal itself and hosted by the groom's parents, can range from an informal barbecue to a formal seven-course meal. If you are planning a more formal event, then all plans and arrangements need to be taken care of well in advance. You should invite all of those who took part in the rehearsal, their spouses or dates (if you desire), out-of-town guests, and the church officiant. Invitations should be sent three weeks ahead of time to all of those involved.

If you feel it is appropriate, establish a seating arrangement with place cards. This allows those who know each other and would be more comfortable sitting together to do so; it also allows you to seat those who are more outgoing with new family and friends so they may become better acquainted. At some point during the dinner, you and your fiancé should make a point of thanking all of those who are participating. This is a perfect time to give a gift to anyone you wish to thank in a very special way.

Before the group disperses, it is important that everyone knows exactly when to meet at the wedding location. It is also a good time to answer any last-minute questions.

For more detailed information on the rehearsal dinner refer to *Wedding Parties and Showers* by Jo Packham.

Rehearsal Dinner Checklist

Rehearsal Dinner Location_____

Contact_____

Address_____

Phone_____

Hours_____

Appointments:_____

Date_____Time_____

Date_____Time_____

Menu_____

_____

_____

Cost per Plate_____

Total Cost_____

The Ceremony Timetable

Prior to the actual day of your wedding, prepare a list and schedule of events to be checked off on the day of the ceremony. Use this to insure that all last-minute details are covered, and that everyone does the right thing at the right time. The following example is based on a formal wedding that is fifteen minutes away from the bride's home. Be certain that any adjustments are made to fit your specific circumstances.

WEDDING MORNING

You, or someone you have selected, should reconfirm plans with the wedding consultant, florist, photographer, and musician(s). Double-check that they know correct times and locations. Make certain the groom has given the bride's wedding ring to the best man.

2 HOURS TO GO

The bride starts dressing with the help of her mother and honor attendant. If the bridesmaids are dressing at home, they should follow the same schedule.

1 HOUR TO GO

Attendants, parents, and bride should meet at the ceremony location for pictures and any last minute details. (If you prefer a very traditional, very formal entrance, then you and your father do not arrive at the church together until ten minutes before the wedding.)The usher, the groomsmen, and the groom should also arrive at the wedding site.

Other members of the wedding party should also begin arriving to receive last minute instructions or offer their help on any last minute details.

45 MINUTES TO GO

The musician(s) begin playing introductory music in the church or on the site. Meanwhile, ushers gather near the entrance and begin escorting guests to their seats, starting with the rows bordering the main aisle, behind those kept for the family.

25 MINUTES TO GO

The clergy member gives any last minute instructions to the groom and ushers, makes certain the marriage license is on hand, and receives his fee from the best man. (For traditional and formal entrances, the bride and her father leave now for the church.)

10 MINUTES TO GO

Wedding party and family go to the vestibule and wait. An usher escorts the grandmothers of the bride to their seats. Another usher escorts the grandmothers of the groom to their seats (with grandfathers following behind). Other relatives are shown to reserved seats. (For a traditional and formal entrance, the bride and her father arrive at the church and join the wedding party.)

5 MINUTES TO GO

The groom's mother is escorted by an usher, with her husband following closely behind, to a seat in the front row on the right side of the church (left, if a Jewish ceremony). Any last minute guests who are waiting are seated. The last person to take her place is the bride's mother. Musical solo begins.

1 MINUTE TO GO

Two ushers lay the aisle runner, if one has been selected. They then return to the vestibule for the procession.

CEREMONY TIME

The officiant takes his position at the front of the church; see page 96. The groom, accompanied by the best man, enters to the front of the altar from a nearby room and stands ready. The processional music now begins.

The Ceremony

Processional

The ushers walk up the aisle in pairs starting with the shortest to the tallest. The bridesmaids follow (in pairs, if there are more than four, or singly, if you choose), also starting with the shortest. If there is an uneven number and you wish them to walk in pairs, have the first attendant walk in singly. The maid-of-honor is next, followed by the ring bearer and flower girl. The ring bearer can walk either before or with the flower girl.

The organist pauses again for a moment to indicate that you and your father are about to enter. The music begins and you slowly walk down the aisle. The guests rise until the officiant asks them to be seated. (Your mother will want to be very aware of this sequence and timing because the other guests will often use her as an indication of when to rise and be seated.) The procession for a Catholic wedding follows the same procedures, except that the bride is not given away. Her father escorts her to the steps of the altar where her groom and the priest are waiting. The father then places his daughter's hand in the groom's hand. He may lift his daughter's veil and kiss her before taking his seat beside his wife.

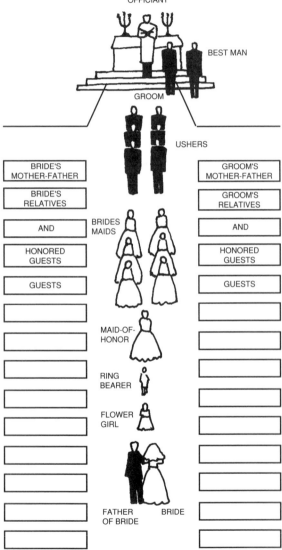

OFFICIANT

BEST MAN

GROOM

USHERS

BRIDE'S
MOTHER-FATHER

BRIDE'S
RELATIVES

AND

HONORED
GUESTS

GUESTS

GROOM'S
MOTHER-FATHER

GROOM'S
RELATIVES

AND

HONORED
GUESTS

GUESTS

BRIDES
MAIDS

MAID-OF-
HONOR

RING
BEARER

FLOWER
GIRL

FATHER
OF BRIDE

BRIDE

At the Altar

The officiant stands at the altar, facing the guests, with you on the left and the groom on the right. The best man stands next to the groom, the ring bearer is next and then the ushers. The maid-of-honor stands next to you and the flower girl stands next to her. The bridesmaids line up next to the flower girl.

To be certain everyone is standing in the right position, you might want to place a penny or a flower petal on the spot where each attendant is to stand. This will avoid crowding.

Recessional

Upon completion of the ceremony, the organist plays as you and the groom walk arm-in-arm down the aisle; see below. The flower girl and ring bearer pair off and follow behind. Then the maid-of-honor and the best man pair off, followed by pairs of the bridesmaids and ushers. The officiant follows the last bridesmaid and usher. You may want to form a receiving line immediately after the ceremony. Your guests will want to give you their congratulations as soon as possible. After the recessional, the ushers return to the ceremony site and escort guests out.

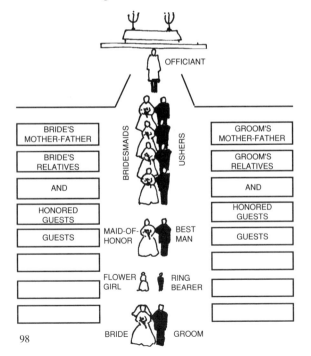

For a Jewish Wedding
Processional

Jewish processionals vary according to custom and to the preference of the family. An example might be:

The beginning of the processional is started off with uplifting music played by the organist. The rabbi is the first to walk down the aisle; he is followed by the ushers. The ushers walk singly, the best man follows. The groom is escorted by both of his parents. The groom's father is on his left and the groom's mother is on his right. The bridesmaids follow single file. The maid-of-honor is next followed by the flower girl and ring bearer. You are escorted by your parents. Your father is also on your left and your mother on your right.

In the most elaborate of Jewish ceremonies (see page 100), the rabbi and cantor are followed by the couple's grandparents, the ushers, the best man, the groom and his parents, the bridesmaids, the bride's honor attendant, ring bearer, flower girl, and then the bride with her parents.

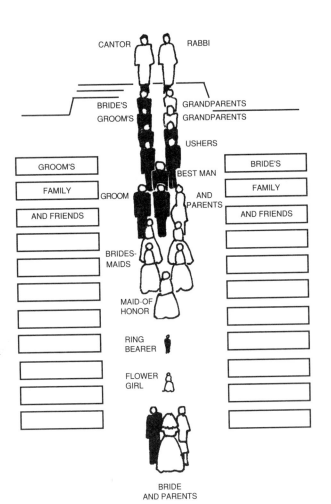

CANTOR   RABBI

BRIDE'S   GRANDPARENTS

GROOM'S   GRANDPARENTS

USHERS

GROOM'S   BRIDE'S

FAMILY   BEST MAN   FAMILY

GROOM   AND

AND FRIENDS   PARENTS   AND FRIENDS

BRIDES-
MAIDS

MAID-OF
HONOR

RING
BEARER

FLOWER
GIRL

BRIDE
AND PARENTS

At the Altar

Both the bride and groom stand with the rabbi under the huppah. The maid-of-honor should be on your right and the groom's best man on his left under the huppah. If room permits under the huppah (see below), the groom's mother and father stand on the left side and your mother and father stand on the right side. If room permits, grandparents may also join under the huppah. The bridesmaids and ushers stand outside of the huppah.

Recessional

You and the groom lead the way down the aisle for the recessional; see below. Your mother and father are next, followed by the groom's mother and father. Then the grandparents exit. The ushers and bridesmaids pair off. The flower girl and ring bearer are next, followed by the rabbi and cantor.

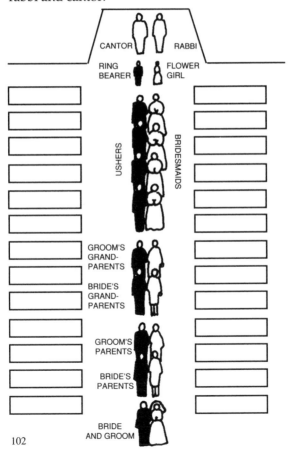

Receiving Line for all Ceremonies

Once the officiant has concluded the ceremony with the pronouncement of marriage, the recessional will follow. Following the recessional procedures that are appropriate for your particular ceremony and circumstances, you and the groom will lead the way down the aisle.

The receiving line should be formed in the vestibule of the church, if the clergy permits (or in an area close to but away from the altar, if the ceremony is not in a church). You may want to consider having only the bride, the groom, and both sets of parents in this receiving line. If there is to be a receiving line at the reception, then all of the attendants may or may not join you at that time. Regardless of your choice, be sure the people you expect to join you are told at the rehearsal. Now family and friends may file through the line offering their best wishes and congratulations.

At informal weddings today, some brides elect not to have a wedding line. This is awkward for guests who have to seek out the bride and groom. At the very least, you and the groom will want to greet your guests together.

Ceremony Transportation

What will it be? A long black limousine or an antique roadster. How about an elegant Mercedes or even a horse and carriage? When it comes to transportation, the options are endless.

Some brides opt for a fleet of chauffeur-driven limousines to make their wedding ultra-elegant, others take a more basic approach and simply arrive or drive away in the family car. Whatever you choose, you and your wedding party will need transportation to the ceremony, to the reception, and from the reception.

Traditionally and formally, the bride rides to the ceremony in one car with her father. Her mother and the maid-of-honor ride in another car. The groom and best man usually occupy still another car, while the remaining attendants ride in separate vehicles.

If you decide to rent a limousine, as with all professional services you hire, you should:

1. Compare rates with several different limousine companies.

2. Ask about the minimum number of hours required for rental.

3. Ask about quantity discounts.

4. Make certain you see the actual limousines that will be used, get proof of insurance from the company, ask about the driver's qualifications and driving record, and discuss proper attire.

5. Get a written contract that specifies the terms of the rental/cancellation policy.
6. Give the driver a list which contains the times everyone is to be picked up, the names and addresses of the people he will be picking up, and the location they are to be taken to.
7. The list should also contain drop-off times, locations, and names.
8. Give the driver a map with explicit directions to each location, plus a name and phone number of someone he can call in the event he gets lost.

The limousine should arrive fifteen minutes early. The driver should be tipped; fifteen percent of the total cost of the rental is customary. The best way to handle this is to place the tip money in an envelope, then ask your father or an usher to pass the money along after the ceremony.

If you have guests flying in from out of town, most of them will need transportation. You might arrange for cab service, or car rental, or have family members pick them up. If family or friends are called on to use their cars for transporting out-of-town guests, make certain you pay for a full tank of gas, give them a small gift, and always send a thank-you note.

Reserve parking spaces at the site of the ceremony for the necessary number of cars.

Transportation Checklist

Name of Firm_____

Address_____

Phone_____

Contact_____

Hours of Rental_____

Deposit_____

Deposit Due Date_____

Contract Signed_____

Number of Vehicles_____

Rental Fee per Hour_____

Total Transportation Costs_____

Driver_____

Ceremony Transportation
Passenger(s)_____

Address_____

Pick-up Time_____

Passenger(s)_____

Address_____

Pick-up Time_____

Passenger(s)_____

Address_____

Pick-up Time_____

Passenger(s)_____

Address_____

Pick-up Time_____

Passenger(s)_____

Address_____

Pick-up Time_____

Passenger(s)_____

Address_____

Pick-up Time_____

Passenger(s)_____

Address_____

Pick-up Time_____

Passenger(s)_____

Address_____

Pick-up Time_____

Ceremony Parking

For large weddings in congested areas or large hotels, parking attendants help ease the confusion and long distance walks to the ceremony. If your wedding coincides with a holiday or a special event, contract with the local police department for possible assistance with traffic control.

If you are hiring independent parking attendants, make certain they are insured and licensed. You are trusting your guests' cars and valuables to these attendants.

Discuss the rates and gratuities. Some companies charge based on the number of guests you have and others on the actual number of cars parked. Negotiate fees for large groups. Inquire about the number of attendants per site. Most companies include gratuities in the fees. If gratuities are prepaid, the parking attendant should post a sign to that effect so guests know.

To love is to choose.

Joseph Poux

Parking Attendant Checklist

Attendant's Name_____

Address_____

Phone_____

Age_____

Driver's License_____

Insurance Company_____

Time of Arrival_____

Time of Departure_____

Attendant's Attire_____

Fees_____

Tips_____

Cancellation Policy_____

Sign Posted if Tip Prepaid_____

Deposit Due/Date_____

Balance Due/Date_____

Index

Altar   97, 101
Buddhist   23
Candlelight ceremony   48
Catholic, Roman   9
Ceremonies, types of   9
Ceremony   95
Ceremony Music   57
Ceremony Parking   108
Ceremony Planning   8
Ceremony Programs   79
Ceremony Rehearsal   83
Ceremony Seating   75
Ceremony Sites   66
Ceremony Styles   30
Ceremony Vows   53
Ceremony Timetable   92
Ceremony Transportation   104
Chapel, wedding   68
Children from first marriage   51
Choosing the Church Officiant   27
Christian Science Church   22
Church   67
Church of Jesus Christ
    of Latter-Day Saints   19
City hall   68
Civil   33
Club   68
Deceased father   51
Double wedding   39
Eastern Orthodox   13
Ecumenical   25, 33
Elopement   42
Escort   50
Formal   30
Home ceremony   69
Hotel   68
Informal   32
Islam   24
Jewish   14, 99
Justice of the peace   68
Latter-Day Saints (Mormon)   19
Lighting of the unity candle   47

Marriage License   *81*
Military ceremony   *37*
Music   *57*
Muslim   *24*
Nondenominational   *26, 33*
Nontraditional   *34*
Officiant   *27, 28*
Older bride   *35*
Outdoors   *70*
Parking   *108*
Personalizing vows   *54*
Planning   *8, 43*
Processional   *95, 99*
Programs   *79*
Protestant   *12*
Quakers   *21*
Reaffirming vows   *36*
Receiving Line for all Ceremonies   *103*
Recessional   *98, 102*
Rectory   *67*
Rehearsal   *83*
Rehearsal dinner   *90*
Religious   *32*
Religious Society of Friends   *21*
Reserved seating   *75, 77*
Restaurant   *68*
Roman Catholic   *9*
Seating   *75*
Second marriages   *36*
Semiformal   *30*
Sites   *66*
Special Circumstances
   Related to the Ceremony   *50*
Styles   *30*
Symbolic Ceremonies   *47*
Synagogue   *67*
Temple   *67*
Timetable   *92*
Traditional   *34*
Transportation   *104*
Types of Ceremonies   *9*
Vows   *53*
Wedding chapel   *68*
Wedding ring ceremony   *47*
Weekend wedding   *41*
Wine ceremony   *47*

*Marriage today must...be concerned not
with the inviolable commitment of constancy and
unending passions, but with the changing patterns
of liberty and discovery.*

Carolyn Heilbrun